I0697779

MILTON ABADIA

BATTLES WITHIN BORDERS

Immigrants tales of lost dreams

Copyright © 2024 by Milton Abadia

All rights reserved. No part of this publication may be reproduced, stored or transmitted in any form or by any means, electronic, mechanical, photocopying, recording, scanning, or otherwise without written permission from the publisher. It is illegal to copy this book, post it to a website, or distribute it by any other means without permission.

Milton Abadia asserts the moral right to be identified as the author of this work.

Milton Abadia has no responsibility for the persistence or accuracy of URLs for external or third-party Internet Websites referred to in this publication and does not guarantee that any content on such Websites is, or will remain, accurate or appropriate.

Designations used by companies to distinguish their products are often claimed as trademarks. All brand names and product names used in this book and on its cover are trade names, service marks, trademarks and registered trademarks of their respective owners. The publishers and the book are not associated with any product or vendor mentioned in this book. None of the companies referenced within the book have endorsed the book.

First edition

This book was professionally typeset on Reedsy.
Find out more at reedsy.com

Contents

1

Introduction

Welcome, dear reader, to the vibrant world of "Battles Within Borders: Immigrant's Tales of Lost Dreams." I'm your guide on this literary journey, Milton Abadia, a Latino with 23 years of experience navigating the complexities of life in the USA. Buckle up as we embark on an exploration of the immigrant experience, a tapestry woven with threads of hope, resilience, and the undeniable charm of the human spirit.

What can you expect from this narrative adventure? Picture a mosaic of stories, each revealing the intricate dance between dreams and reality, painted with hues of humor, curiosity, and rich detail for my experience.

As we delve into the lives of immigrants, we'll traverse the landscapes of diverse journeys, facing the universal challenges of cultural exchange, identity, and the ever-evolving quest for belonging.

But before we dive headfirst into these tales, let's pause for a moment. In this introductory chapter, we'll set the stage, laying the foundation for the narratives that follow. As a fellow traveler in this vast, unpredictable terrain, I invite you to connect with the reality of immigrant experiences—their joys, struggles, and the intricate dance between the past and the present.

So, dear reader, fasten your seat belt, adjust your lens, and join me on this expedition into the heart of immigrant stories. Through the lens of my journey and those of countless others, we'll navigate the winding paths of leaving, arriving, and the perpetual quest for connection in a new world. Get ready for a blend of introspection, humor, and the profound moments that define the immigrant experience.

As we embark on this literary adventure, I promise you an exploration that not only informs but also entertains, leaving you enlightened and perhaps chuckling, often in the very same breath. Let the odyssey begin.

2

From the Past, Only the Experience

Embarking on the tales of immigrants, we find ourselves at the crossroads of history and personal narrative, where each individual carries a unique story shaped by the amalgamation of past experiences and the uncertainty of the future. In this initial chapter, we will navigate the intricate landscape of leaving one's homeland, understanding the subtle nuances between being an immigrant and an emigrant, exploring the multifaceted reasons that propel individuals to traverse borders, and delving into the transformative process of changing one's mental outlook.

Immigrant or Emigrant: Navigating the Spectrum of Movement

Let's first unravel the delicate threads woven into the terms "immigrant" and "emigrant." An immigrant, in its essence, is an adventurer, a dreamer seeking new horizons, opportunities, and the promise of a better life in a foreign land. Contrastingly, an emigrant is one who, driven by necessity or circumstance, bids farewell to the familiar, often in pursuit of safety, escape, or refuge. While the terms may appear interchangeable, they encapsulate the emotional and psychological dimensions of the journey, emphasizing the profound shift in perspective that occurs as one crosses borders.

Reasons to Leave: A Mosaic of Motivations

The decision to leave one's homeland is never a monolithic one; rather, it's a complex tapestry woven from myriad threads of motivation. We will explore the diverse reasons that drive individuals to embark on this transformative journey. From economic hardships and political unrest to the pursuit of education, love, or even the sheer yearning for a different way of life, these narratives will unveil the depth of human desires and the lengths people are willing to go to fulfill them. Each story is a unique window into the compelling forces that lead individuals to set out on a journey into the unknown.

Changing My Mental Chip: A Profound Shift in Perspective

The decision to leave one's homeland not only involves a change of physical location but necessitates a profound transformation in mindset, for sure. We'll delve into the emotional and psychological aspects of the immigrant experience, exploring the complexities of adapting to new cultural norms, and linguistic nuances, and reshaping one's perceptions of self and identity. Through a tapestry of personal anecdotes and shared experiences, we'll illuminate the challenges and triumphs of this internal metamorphosis. Changing one's mental chip is not a static event but a dynamic, ongoing process, marked by introspection, adaptation, and the forging of a new sense of self.

In this chapter, we embark on a journey through the corridors of departure, understanding the choices made and the mental landscapes traversed by those who dare to dream beyond borders. Join me as we navigate the intricate dance between the past and the present, where every step forward is laden with the weight of experience, and every choice made echoes the resilience of the human spirit.

3

Diverse Journeys

Facing the Process

In this section, we delve into the intricate process that immigrants undergo as they navigate the challenges and opportunities presented by a new environment. Picture Maria, a recent immigrant from Mexico, as she grapples with the cultural nuances and language barriers of her new home in the United States.

Through her narratives and shared experiences, we explore the initial stages of adaptation, addressing the cultural, social, and logistical hurdles that individuals like Maria encounter upon arriving in a foreign land. This section aims to provide readers with a vivid portrayal of the early phases of the immigrant journey, capturing the resilience and adaptability required to face the unknown.

- *Culture Shock:* Immigrants often face the initial challenge of adapting to a new culture. From language barriers to unfamiliar social norms, this subsection explores the process of overcoming culture shock.

- *Logistical Hurdles:* Addressing the practical aspects of relocation, such as finding housing, navigating transportation systems, and understanding healthcare, sheds light on the multifaceted challenges immigrants encounter.

Balance Point - Do I Stay or Go?

At the heart of every immigrant's journey lies a crucial crossroads—weighing the decision to stay in their homeland or embark on the uncertain path of immigration. Imagine Ali, torn between the familiarity of his home country and the allure of new possibilities in a foreign land.

This section delves into the internal conflicts, external pressures, and profound considerations that individuals like Ali grapple with when standing at this pivotal balance point. Through personal reflections and real-life stories, we aim to illuminate the complexities of this decision-making process, showcasing the factors that tip the scales in favor of a new beginning or anchor one to familiar shores.

- *Internal Conflicts:* Sharing personal stories of individuals torn between staying in their homeland, rooted in familiarity, and embracing the uncertainties of a new land.
- *External Pressures:* Examining the societal, economic, and political factors that influence the decision-making process, showcasing how external forces play a role in shaping an individual's choice.

Motivation Unveiled

Motivation serves as the driving force behind the decision to leave one's homeland. Meet Aisha, driven by the pursuit of education as she leaves her home in India to study abroad. In this section, we unravel the diverse motivations that propel individuals like Aisha to embark on the transformative journey of immigration. By weaving together stories of economic hardships, political unrest, the pursuit of education, love, and the yearning for a different life, we aim to provide readers with a comprehensive understanding of the myriad factors that influence this life-altering choice.

- *Economic Motivation:* Exploring stories of individuals seeking better economic opportunities, whether to escape poverty or pursue a higher standard of living.
- *Educational Pursuits:* Narratives of those driven by the pursuit of education, showcasing the lengths people go to broaden their horizons and access new learning environments.

Black and White Perspectives

The immigrant experience is a vivid tapestry painted with contrasting emotions, challenges, and triumphs. Join Javier as he experiences the emotional rollercoaster of adapting to a new culture, showcasing the stark contrasts and subtle shades that characterize the immigrant journey.

Through personal narratives, we aim to capture the emotional depth of the experience, showcasing the resilience required to navigate the complexities of adapting to a new culture, forging new identities, and embracing the vivid spectrum of emotions that define the immigrant narrative.

- *Emotional Contrasts:* Highlighting the emotional highs and lows of the immigrant experience, from the excitement of a new beginning to the challenges of leaving behind familiar surroundings.

- *Identity Exploration:* Exploring the transformative journey of identity formation, including the redefinition of self in a new cultural context.

4

Cultural Exchange

Cultural exchange involves the sharing and blending of cultural elements among people from different backgrounds. In this chapter, we explore both the advances and disadvantages associated with cultural exchange, emphasizing the dynamic nature of interactions between diverse communities.

Embracing Diversity

Advances: Cultural exchange fosters a rich tapestry of diversity, enabling individuals to appreciate and celebrate differences. Through exposure to various traditions, cuisines, and perspectives, communities often develop a more inclusive and tolerant mindset. For example, a community festival that showcases diverse cultural performances and cuisines encourages mutual understanding and appreciation among attendees.

Disadvances: However, challenges may arise when cultural exchange is superficial or when cultural elements are appropriated without under-standing their deeper meanings. For instance, adopting a traditional outfit for fashion purposes without recognizing its cultural significance can lead to misrepresentation and stereotyping.

Cross-Cultural Understanding

Advances: Genuine cross-cultural understanding is a significant benefit of cultural exchange. It allows individuals to build meaningful con-nections, fostering mutual respect. An example is a language exchange program where participants not only learn each other's languages but also gain insights into the cultural nuances that shape communication styles and expressions.

Disadvances: On the flip side, misunderstandings can occur when cultural differences are oversimplified or essentialized. This may lead to stereotypes and biases, hindering authentic understanding. For instance, assuming that all individuals from a particular culture share the same beliefs can perpetuate harmful stereotypes.

Culinary Fusion

Advances: Culinary exchange is a delightful aspect of cultural interaction, leading to the fusion of diverse flavors and ingredients. This can result in the creation of new, exciting dishes that reflect the blending of culinary traditions. A food festival where chefs collaborate to create fusion cuisine showcases the positive aspects of culinary exchange.

Disadvances: However, challenges may arise if a culinary exchange is not approached respectfully. Appropriating recipes without acknowledging their origins or commercializing traditional dishes without due credit can lead to cultural insensitivity and erasure.

Artistic Synthesis

Advances: Artistic expression is a powerful avenue for cultural exchange. Collaborations between artists from different cultural backgrounds can lead to the creation of unique and innovative works that bridge artistic traditions. An art exhibition featuring collaborative pieces from artists of diverse backgrounds exemplifies the positive impact of artistic synthesis.

Disadvances: Yet, challenges may emerge if cultural appropriation occurs, where elements of one culture are taken out of context and used without proper understanding or respect. This can lead to the misrepresentation of cultural symbols and traditions.

In each section, the advances represent positive outcomes of cultural exchange, while the disadvantages highlight potential pitfalls or challenges that may arise. Balancing cultural exchange requires a thoughtful and respectful approach to ensure that interactions lead to mutual understanding, appreciation, and enrichment.

5

Identity and Belonging

This chapter delves into the complexities of identity formation and the search for a sense of belonging among immigrants. We explore factors that can shape the future of immigrants, both positively and negatively, as they navigate the intricate landscape of identity and belonging.

Cultural Integration - Positive Impact

Factors Affecting the Future:

Cultural integration positively influences the future of immigrants by fostering a sense of belonging and connection to their adopted community. The degree to which immigrants embrace local customs, traditions, and social norms can significantly impact their long-term integration and acceptance.

Examples:

- **Language Proficiency:** Immigrants who invest in learning the language of their new community often experience enhanced social

13

interactions and professional opportunities.

- **Community Involvement:** Active participation in local events, clubs, or community organizations facilitates a smoother integration process, contributing to a sense of belonging.

Discrimination and Prejudice - Negative Impact

Factors Affecting the Future:

Experiencing discrimination and prejudice can have a detrimental impact on the future of immigrants, influencing their mental well-being, opportunities, and sense of belonging in the long run.

Examples:

- **Job Market Discrimination:** Immigrants facing employment discrimination based on their cultural background may encounter obstacles in career advancement, affecting their economic stability and prospects.

- **Social Exclusion:** Persistent prejudices leading to social exclusion can result in feelings of isolation and hinder the development of a strong social support network, impacting mental health and overall life satisfaction.

Generational Dynamics - Complex Impact

Factors Affecting the Future:

Generational dynamics within immigrant families can shape the future in intricate ways, impacting the transmission of cultural identity, values, and the sense of belonging from one generation to the next.

Examples:

- **Cultural Preservation:** Older generations passing down cultural traditions and values contribute to the preservation of a strong cultural identity among younger family members.

-

- **Generational Conflict:** Differences in cultural adaptation and identity between generations may lead to conflicts, affecting family cohesion and the future trajectory of cultural heritage.

Legal Status and Policies - Varied Impact

Factors Affecting the Future:
Legal status and immigration policies play a crucial role in shaping the future of immigrants, influencing their ability to establish roots, contribute to society, and achieve a sense of belonging.

Examples:

- **Path to Citizenship:** Obtaining legal permanent residency or citizenship provides immigrants with a more stable foundation for building their future, including access to education, employment, and social benefits.

- **Uncertain Immigration Status:** Living with uncertain immigration status can create anxiety, limiting long-term planning, and hindering the development of a secure and stable future.

In each section, the examples illustrate how various factors can either positively or negatively impact the future of immigrants in terms of identity formation and a sense of belonging. The chapter aims to explore the nuanced interplay of these factors and their lasting effects on the immigrant experience.

6

Generational Perspectives

This chapter delves into the distinct perspectives and experiences that different generations within immigrant families bring to the forefront. It explores how the dynamics between first-generation, second-generation, and subsequent generations influence identity, cultural adaptation, and the overall immigrant narrative.

First-Generation Struggles and Triumphs

Perspectives:

First-generation immigrants, often the pioneers in a new land, navigate a unique set of challenges as they adapt to a different culture, language, and societal norms. Their perspectives reflect resilience, determination, and the pursuit of opportunities in a foreign environment.

Examples:

- **Language Barrier Triumphs:** First-generation immigrants may celebrate triumphs in overcoming language barriers, mastering a new language to communicate effectively, and integrating into their adopted society.

- **Professional Accomplishments:** The first generation often takes pride in professional accomplishments, having built careers from the ground up in a new and unfamiliar work environment.

Second-Generation Identity Struggles

Perspectives:

Second-generation immigrants grapple with the dual challenge of reconciling their cultural heritage with the demands of the mainstream society they were born into. Their perspectives reflect a nuanced negotiation of identity and belonging.

Examples:

- **Cultural Hybridity:** Second-generation individuals often navigate a sense of cultural hybridity, blending elements of their heritage with the cultural norms of the society in which they were raised.
- **Inter-Generational Tensions:** Tensions may arise as the second generation seeks to balance cultural expectations from their heritage with the expectations and norms of the society in which they are growing up.

Third-Generation Cultural Navigation

Perspectives:
The perspectives of the third generation may involve a more seamless

integration into the culture of the host country, with a sense of belonging that is deeply rooted in both the immigrant heritage and the mainstream culture.

Examples:

- **Cultural Fluency:** The third generation often exhibits cultural fluency, effortlessly navigating between the customs and traditions of their cultural background and those of the society they were born into.
- **Intergenerational Continuity:** While maintaining a connection to their immigrant roots, the third generation may also contribute to the ongoing evolution of cultural traditions within the family, reflecting a dynamic intergenerational continuum.

Bridging Generational Perspectives

Perspectives:

This section explores the interplay and potential conflicts between different generational perspectives within immigrant families. It delves into the efforts to bridge understanding, foster communication, and build a shared sense of identity that spans across generations.

Examples:

- **Intergenerational Dialogue:** Immigrant families engage in inter-generational dialogues to share experiences, address cultural gaps, and foster mutual understanding between generations.
- **Cultural Celebrations:** Families come together to celebrate cultural festivals and traditions, providing a platform for generational

bonding and the transmission of cultural values.

In each section, the chapter aims to illuminate the unique perspectives and experiences that define each generation within immigrant families. The interplay of struggles, triumphs, identity negotiation, and intergenerational dynamics contributes to the rich tapestry of the immigrant narrative across different generations.

7

Historical Context

This chapter delves into the historical context that shapes the immigrant experience, examining how the past has influenced immigration patterns, policies, and societal attitudes. It explores the origins of immigration, pivotal moments, and the potential implications for the future.

Origins of Immigration

Historical Landscape:

The chapter starts by exploring the origins of immigration, tracing the historical roots that led individuals and communities to embark on journeys to new lands. It examines factors such as economic opportunities, religious freedoms, and political upheavals that prompted migration.

Example:

- **Colonial Immigration to the Americas:** The chapter highlights the early waves of immigration, including European colonization, which shaped the demographic landscape of the Americas and laid the foundation for future waves of migration.

Pivotal Moments in Immigration History

Historical Landscape:

The narrative then shifts to pivotal moments that significantly impacted immigration patterns. This could include events such as wars, economic shifts, or legislative changes that shaped the trajectory of immigration over the years.

Example:

- **Post-World War II Migration:** The chapter explores the surge in immigration post-World War II, driven by economic reconstruction, geopolitical changes, and the need for labor in rebuilding societies.

Evolving Immigration Policies

Historical Landscape:

The chapter delves into the evolution of immigration policies, examining how governments have shaped and regulated migration over time. It explores key legislative acts, policy shifts, and their impacts on immigrant communities.

Example:

- **U.S. Immigration Acts:** The chapter highlights key U.S. immigration acts, such as the Immigration and Nationality Act of 1965, and their role in shaping the demographic composition and diversity of the nation.

Societal Attitudes and Changing Narratives

Historical Landscape:

Examining societal attitudes towards immigrants over different historical periods, this section explores how public perception, cultural norms, and prejudices have influenced the immigrant experience.

Example:

- **Changing Narratives Post-9/11:** The chapter analyzes the shift in societal attitudes towards immigrants, particularly those from certain regions, following the events of September 11, 2001, and the subsequent impact on immigration policies.

The Future of Immigration

Historical Landscape and Speculation:

The chapter concludes by speculating on the potential future of immigration, considering current trends, geopolitical shifts, and societal changes. It addresses how historical context may continue to shape the immigrant experience in the years to come.

Example:

- **Globalization and Migration Trends:** The chapter explores how globalization, climate change, and geopolitical developments may influence future patterns of immigration, shaping the experiences of new generations of immigrants.

By examining the historical context of immigration, this chapter aims to provide readers with a comprehensive understanding of how past events, policies, and societal attitudes have laid the groundwork for the diverse and dynamic immigrant narratives seen today.

8

20 Successful Immigrants in the last 100 years

1. Albert Einstein (1879-1955) - Physicist

Immigration Process:
Fleeing Nazi persecution in 1933, Einstein emigrated from Germany to the United States, settling in Princeton.
Challenges and Pain:
Einstein faced the pain of leaving his homeland due to rising anti-Semitism, and witnessing the horrors of fascism.
Strategies:
He leveraged his intellectual prowess, collaborating on scientific breakthroughs, including contributions to the atomic bomb.
Transformation:
From a persecuted refugee, Einstein became an advocate for civil rights and a symbol of scientific genius.

2. Madeleine Albright (1937-2019) - Diplomat and Politician

Immigration Process:

Albright, born in Czechoslovakia, sought asylum in the U.S. with her family in 1948, escaping Communist rule.

Challenges and Pain:

Facing displacement twice, Albright adjusted to a new culture and political landscape, developing a deep appreciation for democracy.

Strategies:

Her strategy involved academic excellence, obtaining a Ph.D., and leveraging her expertise to become U.S. Secretary of State.

Transformation:

Albright broke gender barriers, leaving a legacy as a skilled diplomat and advocate for democratic values.

3. Malala Yousafzai (1997-present) - Activist and Author

Immigration Process:

Surviving a Taliban assassination attempt, Malala sought asylum in the UK in 2012, where she continues her advocacy.

Challenges and Pain:

Enduring physical and emotional pain, Malala adjusted to a new culture while remaining committed to girls' education.

Strategies:

Her strategy involved using her voice and international platform to advocate for girls' education globally.

Transformation:

From a victim of violence, Malala became a global symbol of resilience and activism.

(Profiles 4-20 follow a similar structure, providing concise details about each individual's immigration journey, strategies employed, challenges faced, and contributions to humanity.)

4. Wyclef Jean (1969-present) - Musician and Activist

Immigration Process:

Fleeing political instability in Haiti, Jean immigrated to the U.S. in the 1980s.

Challenges and Pain:

Adjusting to a new culture, he faced the challenges of poverty and discrimination.

Strategies:

Jean's musical talent became his gateway to success, blending hip-hop and Caribbean influences.

Transformation:

From a struggling immigrant, Jean rose to international fame, using his platform for activism and philanthropy.

5. Isabel Allende (1942-present) - Author

Immigration Process:

Chilean author Allende fled the Pinochet regime in 1973, seeking refuge in Venezuela before settling in the U.S.

Challenges and Pain:

Facing political exile, she navigated the challenges of adapting to a new literary and cultural landscape.

Strategies:

Allende's storytelling skills, rooted in her Latin American heritage, became her strength.

Transformation:

From a political refugee, Allende became a celebrated author, blending magic realism with social and political commentary.

6. Elon Musk (1971-present) - Entrepreneur and Innovator

Immigration Process:

South African-born Musk moved to the U.S. in the 1990s, co-founding companies like PayPal, Tesla, and SpaceX.

Challenges and Pain:

Overcoming financial struggles and initial business failures, Musk faced skepticism in the tech industry.

Strategies:

Musk's visionary approach and relentless pursuit of innovative ideas led to the success of SpaceX and Tesla.

Transformation:

From an immigrant entrepreneur, Musk became a key figure in space exploration and sustainable energy.

7. Gloria Estefan (1957-present) - Singer and Actress

Immigration Process:

Fleeing political unrest in Cuba, Estefan's family immigrated to the U.S. in 1960.

Challenges and Pain:

Facing cultural adjustment and language barriers, Estefan encountered resistance in the music industry.

Strategies:

Her strategy involved embracing her Cuban heritage in her music, leading to international success.

Transformation:
From a young immigrant, Estefan became a Latin music icon, paving the way for others in the industry.

8.   Andrew Ng (1976-present) - Computer Scientist and Entrepreneur

Immigration Process:
Chinese-American Ng moved to the U.S. for graduate studies, later co-founding Google Brain and Coursera.
Challenges and Pain:
Navigating cultural differences and the pressure of academic success, Ng faced the challenges of being an immigrant student.
Strategies:
Ng's strategy involved groundbreaking contributions to artificial intelligence and democratizing education through online platforms.
Transformation:
From an immigrant scholar, Ng became a leading figure in AI research and education.

9. Celia Cruz (1925-2003) - Queen of Salsa

Immigration Process:
Cuban singer Celia Cruz fled the Castro regime in 1960, settling in the U.S.
Challenges and Pain:
Adapting to a new music scene and language, Cruz faced initial resistance in the U.S. music industry.
Strategies:

Cruz's strategy involved infusing Afro-Cuban rhythms into her music, creating a unique salsa sound.

Transformation:

From a Cuban exile, Cruz became the Queen of Salsa, influencing Latin music globally.

10. Sergey Brin (1973-present) - Computer Scientist and Entrepreneur

Immigration Process:

Soviet-born Brin immigrated to the U.S. with his family in 1979, co-founding Google with Larry Page.

Challenges and Pain:

Brin faced cultural adjustment and financial challenges, initially working on Google while pursuing his Ph.D.

Strategies:

His strategy involved innovative thinking and collaboration, leading to the creation of one of the world's leading tech companies.

Transformation:

From a Soviet immigrant, Brin became a tech pioneer, shaping the landscape of online information.

11. George Soros (1930-present) - Investor and Philanthropist

Immigration Process: Fled Hungary for the U.K. and later moved to the U.S. in 1956.

Challenges and Pain: Survived the Nazi occupation and later communism, faced financial struggles.

Achievements and Strategies: Became a successful investor and philanthropist, leveraging financial acumen.

Transformation and Legacy: Transformed into a prominent philanthropist, supporting democracy and human rights.

12. Salman Rushdie (1947-present) - Author

Immigration Process: Moved from India to the U.K. in 1961.

Challenges and Pain: Navigated cultural adaptation and faced threats due to his controversial writing.

Achievements and Strategies: Became a renowned author, leveraging literary contributions.

Transformation and Legacy: Transformed into a literary icon, addressing social and political issues through his works.

13. Haile Gebrselassie (1973-present) - Olympic Runner and Philanthropist

Immigration Process: Moved from Ethiopia to the U.S. for training and competition.

Challenges and Pain: Faced cultural adaptation, language barriers, and financial struggles.

Achievements and Strategies: Became an Olympic gold medalist, leveraging athletic prowess.

Transformation and Legacy: Transformed into a running legend and philanthropist, supporting education and health.

14. Rita Moreno (1931-present) - Actress and Singer

Immigration Process: Moved from Puerto Rico to the U.S. at a young age.

Challenges and Pain: Navigated cultural adaptation, and faced type-casting and stereotypes in Hollywood.

Achievements and Strategies: Became an EGOT winner, leveraging talent and breaking barriers.

Transformation and Legacy: Transformed into an entertainment icon, advocating for diversity in the industry.

15. Yo-Yo Ma (1955-present) - Cellist

Immigration Process: Moved from France to the U.S. as a young child.

Challenges and Pain: Navigated cultural adaptation and language barriers.

Achievements and Strategies: Became a world-renowned cellist, leveraging musical talent.

Transformation and Legacy: Transformed into a classical music virtuoso, promoting cross-cultural understanding.

16. Isabel Dos Santos (1973-present) - Businesswoman

Immigration Process: Moved from Azerbaijan to Angola at a young age.

Challenges and Pain: Navigated cultural adaptation and faced scrutiny for business dealings.

Achievements and Strategies: Became a successful businesswoman, leveraging entrepreneurial skills.

Transformation and Legacy: Transformed into a prominent figure in African business, with a complex legacy.

17. Yusra Mardini (1998-present) - Olympic Swimmer and Refugee

Advocate

Immigration Process: Fled Syria and sought asylum in Germany.

Challenges and Pain: Survived a perilous journey and adjusted to a new culture.

Achievements and Strategies: Became an Olympic swimmer, leveraging athletic talent for refugee advocacy.

Transformation and Legacy: Transformed into a symbol of resilience, advocating for refugee rights.

18. Andrew Carnegie (1835-1919) - Industrialist and Philanthropist

Immigration Process: Moved from Scotland to the U.S. in 1848.

Challenges and Pain: Faced poverty as an immigrant, and worked his way up in the steel industry.

Achievements and Strategies: Became an industrial tycoon, leveraging business acumen.

Transformation and Legacy: Transformed into a philanthropist, supporting education and libraries.

19. Carlos Santana (1947-present) - Musician

Immigration Process: Moved from Mexico to the U.S. as a child.

Challenges and Pain: Navigated cultural adaptation and financial struggles.

Achievements and Strategies: Became a Grammy-winning musician, leveraging musical talent.

Transformation and Legacy: Transformed into a guitar legend, blending

Latin and rock music.

20. Zhang Xin (1965-present) - Real Estate Mogul

Immigration Process: Moved from China to the U.K. for studies and later to the U.S.

Challenges and Pain: Navigated cultural adaptation and financial struggles.

Achievements and Strategies: Became a real estate mogul, leveraging entrepreneurship.

Transformation and Legacy: Transformed into a prominent figure in global real estate.

These stories showcase the diverse experiences of immigrants who overcame challenges, leveraged their strengths, and left lasting legacies in their respective fields.

The story continues and the best thing that could happen is to find your name in the next edition.

9

10 Common Factors to Success

This chapter explores key elements that consistently contribute to the success of immigrants across diverse fields. These common factors highlight the shared characteristics and strategies that have propelled individuals to achieve remarkable accomplishments in their adopted countries.

1. Resilience and Perseverance

Successful immigrants often exhibit a remarkable level of resilience, facing setbacks and challenges with unwavering determination. The ability to persevere in the face of adversity is a common thread in their stories, allowing them to overcome obstacles and continue pursuing their goals.

2. Adaptability and Cultural Fluency

Adaptability is a crucial factor in the success of immigrants. Those who thrive often demonstrate a willingness to adapt to new cultures, languages, and societal norms. Cultural fluency enables effective navigation of diverse environments, fostering a sense of belonging and facilitating professional and personal growth.

3. Educational Pursuits

Many successful immigrants prioritize education as a pathway to success. Whether through formal education or continuous self-learning, a commitment to acquiring knowledge and skills opens doors to opportunities and enhances their ability to contribute meaningfully to society.

4. Networking and Community Engagement

Building strong networks and actively engaging with communities are common strategies among successful immigrants. Establishing connections provides support, mentorship, and access to valuable resources, fostering professional and personal growth.

5. Entrepreneurial Spirit

A significant number of successful immigrants exhibit an entrepreneurial spirit. Whether through founding businesses, investing, or pursuing innovative ventures, they leverage their creativity and determination to make a positive impact and contribute to the economic landscape of their adopted countries.

6. Goal Setting and Strategic Planning

The ability to set clear goals and develop strategic plans is a shared characteristic among successful immigrants. This forward-thinking approach enables them to navigate their journeys with purpose, making informed decisions that align with their long-term aspirations.

7. Embracing Diversity and Inclusion

Successful immigrants often appreciate the value of diversity and inclusion. They contribute to the richness of cultural landscapes, promoting inclusivity and bridging gaps between communities. This mindset fosters collaboration and strengthens social bonds.

8. Strong Work Ethic

A strong work ethic is a common denominator in the success of immigrants. Many demonstrate a commitment to hard work, dedication, and a willingness to go above and beyond to achieve their goals. This work ethic contributes to their professional achievements and societal contributions.

9. Financial Literacy and Planning

Understanding financial principles and planning for the future are key factors in the success of immigrants. Those who manage their finances wisely and make informed investment decisions are better positioned to navigate economic challenges and build a secure future.

10. Giving Back and Philanthropy

Successful immigrants often engage in giving back to their communities and contribute to philanthropic endeavors. This commitment to social responsibility reflects a desire to make a positive impact beyond personal success, leaving a lasting legacy of generosity and compassion.

By exploring these 10 common factors to success, this chapter aims to provide insights into the qualities and strategies that contribute to the achievements of immigrants across various fields and backgrounds.

10

25 Funny Stories about Immigrants

This chapter is dedicated to showcasing the lighter side of the immigrant experience, sharing amusing anecdotes that highlight the humor, resilience, and cultural clashes that often accompany the journey of making a new home in a foreign land.

1. Lost in Translation

An immigrant, still learning English, once confused "construction" with "destruction." Hilarity ensued when they enthusiastically told a friend about the "destruction" happening in their neighborhood.

2. The Grocery Store Mishap

Attempting to buy spaghetti sauce, an immigrant spent an embarrassing amount of time searching for "tomato gravy" at the grocery store, convinced it was the American term.

3. The Alarm Clock Incident

In an attempt to set an alarm for an early morning, an immigrant mistakenly programmed their coffee maker instead. They woke up to a fresh pot of coffee but missed the meeting entirely.

4. The Weather Misunderstanding

Coming from a warmer climate, an immigrant was puzzled by the term "wind chill." Believing it was an actual person, they wondered why Wind Chill was always so unfriendly in winter.

5. The Confused Commute

A new immigrant, accustomed to driving on the left side of the road, found themselves nervously hugging the left curb while driving in a country that drives on the right. It took a few honks to adjust.

6. The Over Enthusiastic Thanksgiving

Not understanding the concept of Thanksgiving, an immigrant prepared an extravagant turkey dinner in July, thinking it was a monthly American tradition.

7. The Elevator Saga

Unfamiliar with the American way of greeting strangers in elevators, an immigrant enthusiastically started conversations with fellow passengers, leading to awkward yet amusing encounters.

8. The Peculiar Pronunciation

An immigrant, trying to fit in at work, mispronounced the word "yogurt" for months until a colleague kindly corrected them. The entire office had a good laugh about the "yo-gurt" era.

9. The Apartment Number Mystery

An immigrant, still getting used to the American address system, once invited friends to the wrong apartment for a dinner party. The neighbors were surprised but graciously joined the festivities.

10. The Confounding Slang

Attempting to use local slang, an immigrant complimented a colleague's "sick" outfit, unaware that it meant impressive, not unwell.

11. The Coffee Shop Challenge

Ordered a "small coffee" and was bewildered by the range of size options. Faced with choices like tall, grande, and venti, the immigrant jokingly asked for a "normal" size.

12. The Ice Cream Mishap

Misunderstanding the concept of "Rocky Road" ice cream, an immigrant excitedly told friends about their adventurous journey to find a street named Rocky Road.

13. The Reverse Seasonal Wardrobe

Coming from the Southern Hemisphere, an immigrant packed winter clothes for a summer move, leading to some funny fashion choices in the scorching heat.

14. The Sneezing Conundrum

Unfamiliar with the American custom of saying "bless you" after a sneeze, an immigrant initially thought people were genuinely concerned about their health.

15. The Phone Number Puzzle

Confused by the American phone number format, an immigrant once tried to call 9-1-1, thinking it was a standard telephone number. The friendly dispatcher patiently explained its purpose.

16. The Ice Cream Truck Excitement

Mistaking the jingle of an ice cream truck for an emergency vehicle, an immigrant once cleared the road to make way for it, much to the amusement of neighbors.

17. The Lawn Care Misadventure

Not understanding the obsession with well-manicured lawns, an immigrant once spent hours meticulously picking up leaves, only to be informed that it's an endless task in fall.

18. The Thanksgiving Turkey Challenge

Puzzled by the enormity of Thanksgiving turkeys, an immigrant attempted to cook one, only to realize it wouldn't fit in their oven. The journey to find a smaller turkey ensued.

19. The Street Crossing Dilemma

Accustomed to more relaxed traffic rules, an immigrant struggled to understand when it was safe to cross the street without a crosswalk signal, leading to comical dance moves at intersections.

20. The Misadventures in Grocery Shopping

Confused by the vast array of breakfast cereals, an immigrant once bought cat food, thinking it was a popular American snack due to the colorful packaging.

21. The Sock Drawer Surprise

Discovering the concept of mismatched socks, an immigrant initially thought it was a fashion statement and proudly wore mismatched socks to a formal event.

22. The Public Transportation Comedy

Not familiar with public transportation etiquette, an immigrant once pulled the bus cord to request a stop and shouted, "Ding, ding," thinking it was the customary signal.

23. The Lawn Chair Encounter

In an attempt to socialize, an immigrant attended a neighborhood BBQ with a folding lawn chair, not realizing it was a casual gathering on the grass.

24. The Ice Cream Flavor Fiasco

Misinterpreting the term "Neapolitan ice cream," an immigrant excitedly shared stories about a new Italian ice cream flavor called "Napoleon."

25. The Thermometer Confusion

Trying to understand Fahrenheit, an immigrant once wore a winter coat in 60-degree weather, convinced it was freezing based on the Celsius scale.

45

These lighthearted stories aim to bring a smile to readers' faces, celebrating the humorous moments that often accompany the immigrant experience.

11

Conclusion

Embracing the American Dream

In the bustling tapestry of my life as a Latin immigrant, I find myself intricately woven into the fabric of the American Dream. Every thread tells a story — a story of resilience, family, business, and the relentless pursuit of dreams.

As I reflect on the journey that brought me across borders, I see the indomitable spirit that guided me through unfamiliar landscapes, echoing the footsteps of countless dreamers who sought a better life. The challenges were formidable, the adjustments profound, yet each hurdle became a stepping stone, propelling me forward.

Family, the Pillar of Strength:

Amidst the hustle and bustle, my family stands tall as the unwavering pillar of my existence. The laughter around the dinner table, the shared joys, and the collective strength in times of adversity embody the essence of my immigrant experience. The bonds formed in the crucible of adaptation are unbreakable, a testament to the enduring power of familial love.

Business Ventures and Ambitions:

In the bustling marketplace of opportunity, I embarked on business ventures, navigating the nuances of entrepreneurship with determination. From the vibrant bodegas to the entrepreneurial dreams that took root, each endeavor told a story of economic aspiration, ambition, and the pursuit of success in the land of opportunity.

Conquering Dreams Every Day:

Every dawn brings with it the promise of new conquests. The dreams I chase are not ephemeral wisps but robust aspirations, born from the fusion of passion and persistence. In this pursuit, I join the chorus of dreamers who have come before me, inspired by the belief that hard work and dedication can transform dreams into reality.

Cultural Tapestry and Identity:

My Latin roots remain deeply embedded in the soil of my identity, enriching the cultural tapestry that defines me. The fusion of traditions, languages, and flavors creates a vibrant mosaic, a testament to the beautiful amalgamation of diverse influences that is the hallmark of the American experience.

The American Dream Unfolds:

As I stand at the intersection of heritage and aspiration, I realize that the American Dream is not a solitary quest but a collective narrative. It is the sum of our stories, each contributing a unique hue to the canvas of possibilities. The dream is not static; it evolves with each generation, with each immigrant who brings their hopes and ambitions to this land.

In concluding this chapter of my immigrant journey, I find solace in the realization that the pursuit of dreams is a lifelong voyage. The challenges are met with resilience, the victories are celebrated with gratitude. The American Dream, elusive yet tangible, remains a beacon, guiding me and countless others toward a future where the pursuit of happiness is not just an ideal but a lived reality.

As the sun sets on each day, I continue to conquer my dreams, not merely for myself but for the generations that will inherit the legacy of this immigrant odyssey. The journey is ongoing, the dreams ever-expanding, and the spirit unwavering — for in the heart of every immigrant, beats the rhythm of a dream that knows no borders.

If you found this book helpful, I'd be very appreciative if you left a favorable review for the book on Amazon!

www.ingramcontent.com/pod-product-compliance
Lightning Source LLC
Chambersburg PA
CBHW070214260726
48658CB00006BA/2076

9798877687639